I WOULD

TELL

YOU A

SECRET

I WOULD TELL YOU A SECRET

POEMS BY
HAYDEN DANSKY

atmosphere press

Published by Atmosphere Press

Cover design by Beste Miray Doğan

atmospherepress.com

TABLE OF CONTENTS

I.

I WOULD TELL YOU A SECRET

I would tell you a secret
but I don't remember most
and since my bones don't talk
I'll have to walk you to their graves,
hold your hand
to remind me now
is far from yesterday
and their flesh was buried
that distance times 100,000,
their secrets buried long before that

I would tell you where we are going
but I don't remember
and my gut can't talk
and the smell of moist leaves
and chilling October air
reminds me where to turn
when I reach it

I would tell you what we are doing here
but I can't remember why I came
and my mind is somewhere in 1997
and I'm pretty sure the answer
is strongly not recommended
by mental health professionals anyway

I would tell you how I used to come here
and curl up on the ground,
fall asleep to the sound of
my solo beating heart
praying for anything less permanent
than the absence of their breath,
any answer less real

than the grief in my bones

I would tell you how I came here
but I can only show you how I slept
in the afternoons,
grass for a sheet,
gravestone for a pillow

I would tell you what she told me before she died
but I promised not to tell anyone
and it was one more compulsive lie,
a mother's sense of control in a crumbling world
I would tell you if
her ghost could apologize
and promise to visit again soon

I would explain to you what's pouring out
but I honestly don't know
Like these tears understand more
than my prefrontal cortex
Like this snot holds more
than any word I've ever known
Like this gasping breath when I finally found them here,
stones covered in falling leaves

I trace my hands amongst the metal edge
of their etched out names
Retrace my new name
where it should say
"Mother of Hayden"
There was so much more I couldn't have known
than just my name
when their hearts stopped

I would tell you what I did know
but my mouth is sealed by tragedy

Stay here with me in silence
until I can move again
Until I can find the power to stand
and walk away
and find today
in your hand

SILENCE

My silence is fire
My silence is a tree
that grows
from a grave,
a snapdragon
with no snap
It's the existential angst of
a grief survivor
a suicide survivor
a lost one finding home again

My silence is a forgotten child
picking up broken branches
to keep the fire alive
so strong it's already
burnt the hearts
of the trees,
a child with not enough
hands to catch
all the falling leaves

My silence is longing
My silence is trauma
My silence is shame
My silence is responsible for the perpetuation of supremacy
My silence is responsible for the impossible

My disposition is fire
My silence and my disposition are
best friends, walk hand in hand through
fields of white orchids,
my silence
knows them well

My silence is intricate
nuanced,
beautiful
A teacher of the world
I never learned
A space to hold
the tears
I never released

My silence is darkness
My silence is laughter
My silence runs through me like
the chaos I always
seem to attract

My silence is complex,
an integration of
faded memories and blurred existence
A room with all of the answers
trapped behind
locked doors
My silence threw away the keys
My disposition knows the answers
My silence keeps my secrets
My secrets keep my chains
My chains keep the birdcage locked
I once knew a free dove who died

OCTOBER SECOND

When the prairie grass turns purple
and the leaves hide
their failures in the rocks
When the seed pods hang
their heads and the crabapples flatten
their faces,
the veil between
my world
and hers thins

Fragility failed me in getting dressed today
Six shirts later
I still have hips,
a uterus,
a soft voice, and a gentle smile
my mother dreamed up for me before
I learned I'm too much

Compulsive pacing morning,
remember how I used to walk
the living room rug
in circles
until she woke up and forgave me for
my naive dissociation?
Compulsive pacing morning,
kiss me like love once did before
it left for Georgia,
like a long walk up
a dirt hill to check the mail,
like a hand
on my back
to bring me home again

My body is a freak child born
to a world of two boxes meant
for strangers
with a users manual
describing something
not in front of me,
with a roadmap to heaven
for only the powerful
addicted to power
My body is breath that science said
should have been dead long ago
My journal is a to-do list
My suicide note, an apology

But I know I'm failing
at a fucking miracle
Again
Today

On October 2nd, 1997, I wonder
what mother had to say
or if she bound her words in liquor that day,
or if she went to rehab that day,
or if she tried harder that day,
or if she thought she may live through it,
or if she knew hope was a lie that day
Or if death peeked its head around the
reddening maples and whispered
instructions to make her
final parting gifts

I wonder if she knew that
she couldn't fail her miracle life

I wonder if I can know that
I'll both never arrive
and let my body be the process
it craves without fear that
she will never return
because it is
too wrong for this world

I wonder if I can thank her ghost
for its soft embrace
in the night before
my bad body turns to ash

SNAPPING TURTLE

When my head tells me I have nothing good to say,
that I'm not worthy of space,
that I don't know enough to speak
When it says to just go home and let this one be,
I pray
to find the confidence to rip my teeth apart,
let my tongue dance with the roof of my mouth
and scream down the sound of
"you can't let them know"

I close my eyes so I can remember
the morning I awoke and said
I cannot do it anymore,
laid down on my floor
shaking so violently I didn't move for three days
because if I told somebody
they just might say
that things will always be this way
and I'm alone in it

It's that feeling of being so uncomfortable
in my own skin
that there's no other explanation but
the demons slithering within
attempting to find their own escape route –
like the same escape I took
the day before I awoke,
my clothes still reeking of liquor
the same smell of my ma's lies, my dad's grip
the way I held on to the fabrics of life
not quite living but
too afraid to die

But the snapping turtle has a heart
that can beat
for up to 8 hours after
it has been killed
Hummingbirds have hearts that
beat one thousand times
a minute
Giraffes have multiple valves up their necks to get
the blood all the way up to their heads
Dogs have the largest hearts
compared to their body size than any other mammal
Octopuses have three

We all just adapt to what we need and
some of us were born with
a fist-sized hole in our gut
we've been shoving booze and people into
so we won't let you see –
some of us were born dying,
but our hearts kept beating

And as our souls wither away
our hearts kept beating
Resilience heard whispers of this kind of strength
So when the whiskey cannons finally fade in
the silence of the rooms
we hear our hearts beat in unison and we know
it's better to open our mouths
and let the harmony come out
just incase
one person feels the same

When they know what I mean when
my words shiver down their veins
and they feel held for just a minute but
that minute is just enough –

I wrote this for you
To the person,
who has taken far too many drinks than
the ones that they mean,
this one is for you
To the person,
who knows they shouldn't take it but
watches as their hand
reaches for another
disconnected from their mind,
wondering how things could possibly be this way.
To the person,
who does lines of coke to keep their body straight up
just to keep the alcohol down
To the person,
who has played spin the bottle with
a bottle of gin, a gun, and a phone
To the person,
who hides narcotics in their room for
years after they quit using
just for an extra sense of security
like a blanket in case
the feelings decide to choose
cold today

To the dogs that clipped their own leashes
To the birds who built their own cages
To the ones who want to do good but
trouble just keeps knocking

To the ones who were born dying
but our hearts kept beating,
laughter will roar through us

We will hold it like it's sacred
Like we hold baskets of
dog licks and red buds
mysteries and miracles
grace and forgiveness
and we will dance with you
It's for you I will find the courage to tell my head to go away
open my mouth and ask
if you want to dance with me too,
it's for the snapping turtles,
just misunderstood

WRITE LIKE YOUR BODY

Don't write like someone has to read it
That's a choice for
a nonexistent moment
you may or may not
ever make it to

Write like your body cannot breathe anymore,
like your heart was crushed under
centuries of genocide,
like your body arrived
on stolen land,
exists in the contradiction
of loving

Write like you were told that your fundamental truth
is simultaneously nonexistent and a sin,
like your body won't fit into this binary,
squeezing its way in and out
between safety and freedom
as if safety and freedom cannot exist in the same room
Write of the longing you have
for everybody
to have safety and freedom
exist in the same room

Write like you know your body holds space
in the way that it does
because you were born white in a dying world
because you were born white
after your grandparents worked so hard
to gift it to you –
You cannot blame them for assimilation
Imagine watching your people burn

staring at your child not knowing
if this world will die
before they do
Can assimilation be resilience instead of apathy?

Write like it could
because your body contorts to male or female to survive
like when you grew out your mustache you hate
before you went to Montana
just in case

Write like you cannot breathe
knowing someone looks at their child every day
wondering if they will
survive in a police state,
like you cannot breathe knowing
that the question up for debate
is whether or not some body matters

This is not a question up for debate
The question up for debate is
whether or not god and despair can exist in the same room?

Write like you are no longer
a bag of lungs
making it through this world but
a body deserving of space
Raised fist
moving to
beating drums
chants
Demanding
something not worth debating
A beating heart
feeling all of this

Write like you know
what an honor it is to be
heartbroken these days

GRAVE NAP

On the nights
with no degrees left
I tremble when
I think of you
cold and alone lying
on the dark earth where
her bones lay to rest
beside the bones of
her first son

I know you went there
as soon as you were
old enough to drive,
16 and your license was your
ticket to the graveyard
Finally free
to be alone
in your obsession
Finally free
to grieve

Dear child, and you were
a child
When your brother
was this age
he was your parent,
died a child

You can fall
asleep with your family
every night

if you want to
think of them
before you dream

You do not have
to remember where
their flesh was buried
so long as you
let yourself melt
into their ghostly embrace

You can fall
asleep alone
if you want to
give yourself rest
from the memories
squeezing themselves
into your head

You can carry
yourself as you
wake in this world
if you want to
regulate yourself
help yourself
hold yourself
But you will never be
held by your mother again

Your truth is in death
where your mind
will never go
Let that be true for
just tonight

Dream softly of
all that is left
on this earth
waiting
to decay

HAND-STITCHED MEMORIES

I.

When I put down my weapons
I see the ghost of you
here as my comrade
even though I've been firing at you
with no flesh
in hopes that I could feel myself in mine
In hopes of making sense
of the time that you had skin too
and yours met mine with a vengeance

I've been carefully stitching a quilt for a flag
from pieces of my torn white t-shirts
that I wear every day
waiting for the anniversary
of your last breath
and my brother's too
although we all know his was yours
even though your body lingered on earth
for three more weeks

My therapist says I get a free pass
to be as messy as I want
from mid-October to the end of November every year for the rest
of my life
My critic says it's impossible
My ego says it doesn't matter
My heart says don't crumble, don't crumble, don't crumble
My desire says to finish the flag
My hands say don't stop stitching

These cracked and dry hands

That have been picking through
A shoebox of memories
desperately searching for just one
to add to this quilt
Just one where
we weren't fighting
Imagining what it would be like
if this box never happened,
and I could hit call on my phone
next to your face,
Hear your old and fading voice
call me by my real name

I don't know what you would have needed to stay on this earth
to leave your black and white desperation behind:
Be drunk or be damned
Be killed or kill yourself
Be fire or burn out
Be fire be fire be fire
Don't crumble don't crumble don't crumble

I wish you could squeeze me so hard
my constrained arms cannot fight you anymore
Love me so hard
you smash the grey out of love,
wear it in your hair instead

But I've been full-on fantasy,
avoiding a vast emptiness consuming me
since the day I scratched the makeup off your cold dead face,
picked it from my tiny fingernails,
kissed your forehead
and watched your body begin its decay

All of a sudden now I'm looking down
at this black hole expanding from my chest

Wondering why I was granted a life
whose work is finding fullness
despite a gaping wound with edges
too jaded for any
other piece to fit
But knowing why not,
because this is the exact thing I've been working towards
This moment of completely crumbling
I'm supposed to just trust fall in to this grief
but I can't crumble, can't crumble, can't crumble

II.

I've been trying to surrender this grief
it's just not ready to surrender me
My body is a vessel for it
almost ready to move
but stuck between a few childhood souvenirs collecting dust
under years worth of torn flesh
heavy breath
My mouth is not yours anymore

But I still can't pry it open
when I see what these hands are holding,
needle and thread,
a white shirt and old photo,
a tiny shoebox of only memories
of both of us trapped
at the bottom of the wishing wells
we built for one another

I've been full-on fantasy but I know
the entire reality of our lives is a precise moment between
memory and imagination
that's too hot to touch,

too full to believe,
too vulnerable to accept

The edges close in on this breath
find love waiting
still

Grief is not an absence of love,
it is love at its fullest
It is loving your ghost
It is love with no place to go

You died 22 years ago
on a highway close to home
Feels like not too long ago
when you called me the wrong name
held me in your bed
listening to the whippoorwills
sing in the eye of the hurricane,
telling me sometimes we just have to
surrender and wait
for the storm to return

GHOST STORY

I told you it was a dream
so you could digest it easier
So you could taste it
before you spit it out
So you would swallow it
before you regurgitated
its untruth back to me
but my whole life I've been a secret keeper

I picked it up from my mother,
watched her as she hid her secrets
in her pockets with her keys,
in the bottom of a bottle of booze
I found them
shoved into envelopes
shoved into books
in the basement library before
I even knew how to read
Secrets shoved into my veins
have become a part of me
and I'm afraid of what you would really think if
I told you it wasn't a dream

That I keep myself awake
on long nights
waiting for her
to come visit me
and she finally looks healthy
and she carries so much beauty

She tells me that when we die
our secrets diminish
She sings me ghostly melodies

until I fall asleep
She says she'll show up
for me this time
like she couldn't in her life
because a ghost is a second chance,

a nightmare waiting to morph
into a new reality,
a fallen star trying to
glow from the ground up
like a seed
I beg her to stay up with me

To tell me of her stories drained from existence with
the softening of her beating heart,
to tell me what she really thinks
without her chains of denial,
her handcuffs of abuse,
without her muffled screams
drowned out by the silence necessary
to keep her addiction alive
To tell me of the world she imagined
when she gave me life,
of her dreams wrapped
with her graying hair,
kissed with a time
she would no longer care
what people think of her,
what they think of me

I beg her to whisper
her secrets of secrets,
the ones we no longer have to keep,
the ones we can let slip between our fingers,
the ones we let slip
on the day that she died and

the first time I surrendered

I ask her why the moon has to wane and
how I can trust it will come back this time?
Why her arms had to be buried and
how I can trust that I will ever find
another mother to hold me?
I ask her to hold me

but her body fades away from mine
Her eyes vanish
like they once did in life,
like her stories with no backbone,
like my secrets with no truth
I want to tell you but
I'm afraid of what you would really think
if I told you it wasn't a dream

FALLING FOR NOTHING

It's 3 am
your heart is in
your throat
again,
your stomach,
some mix between
hungry and nauseous and no
quantity of thinking will
make it go away

You've crossed oceans wondering,
found forests full of questions,
held hope to debate existence
amongst desert plateaus
while watching storms
approach softly
from yesterday
You've taken each step
towards justice
in this cruel and mysterious
world, found yourself
in the heat of fire
demanding another world

This question is no different
than the rest of them
The ones with no right answer
The ones with no answer
The ones that keep
us moving
forward in search
for truth
The ones that terrify

us into stagnation,
hold us
trembling in the night

Find space to hold
the question like
your deepest love,
your own child,
your best friend
May you fall for self-doubt tonight
May you caress your fear
like your last chance to
say what you can
to your lover
when she drifts
off to sleep

Let yourself fall
for the questions
Let yourself crush
for them
Be crushed
Let yourself long
for the chance
you will hold them
again
Fall for the questions,
and yourself,
and your courage
Fall into them
and rest gently
tonight knowing
they will be
by your side
again
tomorrow

II.

THE MOST HOLY THING

To be named a child
with no concept of life
was to use the edges of
a world not meant for me
to carve out my flesh

To be named again
in truth,
was the most holy thing
I ever gave myself

Name me again and again
until I can see how you see
Until I feel my heart
beating in my throat
to remind me
of a mortality
outside of a name
that is mine
permanently contingent
on my desire

Call me again and again
until I know you want me
Until I can feel myself as whole
as the time
at the top of the hill
at the graveyard
when my heart still beat
unlike
hers

Tell me who I am
so I can become defiant,
so I can rant for the sake of ranting,
so I can argue with you,
so I can be the mischief-maker
that you know
only wants to be seen

Name me how you see me;
permit me to change
Love me how you love me;
grant us both the freedom to love everything
Hold me like a motherless child tonight;
let me go tomorrow
to gather more names
and come home
with a few
to try on
so you can tell me
what you think
of me now

TURMERIC

I say I don't trust you
but I'm lying as
I sit in the absurdity of
completing my therapy
homework that you assigned with
my fingers wrapped
around a turmeric chai latte with
coconut almond milk
as if my life was
dependent upon it

As if my sobriety was
dependent upon it
As if these
yellow bubbles popping
against the glass
contained my only
chance of hope
of healing, one day

As if my mother's
one last dying wish
was to see me
keep breathing
long enough
to enjoy a yellow
drink alone
and keep my mind about me

As if the day
I stood by her coffin
and reached
my soft and tiny

hand to her face
to use my fingernails
to scrape off the layers
of makeup
they covered her with,
to hide the dead
from their scars,
so they could
perpetuate the secrets necessary to
keep her dysfunction alive
long after she died,
was yesterday,
and the collapse never came

As if 21 years of
survivors guilt
would melt
under the spice
of the ginger
on my tongue

As if the ancient wisdom
of this turmeric
could be inherited
in any other way
than through the yellow teeth
of a crooked smile
of another person
telling me their life
just like my own,
but with faith
that I too could become

I say I don't trust you
but I'm drinking gold from a cup
and I've never once cared about gold,

but I'd do anything for freedom

I'd do anything
for freedom, which
you seem to carry
around like you have an
endless supply of it
that you'd let fall
from your pockets on purpose
so I could pick some up
for a while

I seem to want to do
anything for freedom
but say
I trust you,

and wait

SCARCITY

I got these pens
that I like again
Worth the $4
for 3 pens
to feel like I can write
as fast as my fingers need,
like nothing's holding them back
from producing nothing
worth sharing
but everything
worth pouring out

Scarcity is a function of the brain
I've had since my body was scarce
When my grandmother
tossed it in the pot
as she taught us to gamble,
dreidel in hand,
"I'll see your two pennies
and raise you
with two more
generations worth of
never enough"
I won that hand
"I'll match your chocolate coins
with one secret
and one denial
It's your turn to spin"
Gimmel

I'm at the store staring at numbers
like my life depends on
the lowest ones,

like the eviction notice will come again,
and we're going to lose the house again,
and I'm going to wake up
on a roof in
Austin, Texas
covered in blood
wondering how
that last bender
got me down here again

Staring down pens
in a hallway
of a corporate store
in a system where they took
everything away
that we needed to survive
to make us work for it back,
wondering if I should work
for this back

Where I exchange dollars
for a life worth living
Where I exchange time
for an art that brings me more time
I'll give you some
minutes of my life
to keep the rest of my life
because my healing
is contingent
on this simple sport of
letting my hand slide
across the page
with ink and a little
judgment attached

I'll give you $4
for the pens
if you give me
$1 for my word
Another $1 for the poem
A head
full of critique
Your turn to spin

DISHES

Staring at the sink
I let my head fall forward,
eyes gazed upon
the pile of dishes
in front of me

If these sponges didn't smell so bad
I would prefer them
If they were not laying around
in sopping messes of themselves
like a typical
depressive Thursday morning
when I cannot get out of bed

If they weren't used
over and over
to scrape the grime off
of our trickle-down leftovers,
the waxy coats
of sauces stuck
on to these plates for dear life
Where no sponge,
no matter how rough,
can actually succeed

I grab the brush waiting for me
but these dishes are just a way out again
Pile them high so I can stand here again
Let my hands do the movement
so I can lose myself again,
so I can leave again

I'm 6 again
and my mother is back
I'm 12 again
Fuck that,
I'm 6 again
Fuck that,
if I can just figure out
what went wrong
Why I didn't know then
Why I must have not
helped enough
cleaned enough
done the dishes enough

If I could just name
what was wrong with me
she would come back to me
If I could have just
been a better child
If I could have just
made sure to wipe
down the sink too
that I could barely reach,
my tiny hands,
and the stool
that was left
around the house
to help me get my head
above the water
If I could have just reached,
she would come back to me

If I could just
get these dishes
to be clean

If I could just
get these dishes
to be clean

If I could just
get these dishes
to be clean

OCD

There is no amount of willpower
that can get me to calm again
I'm therapy-day-stimulated
Manic minus five
I'm six shirts deep and
I'm still too dirty
Two showers in and
I didn't scrub hard enough

I've already
taken out the trash
swept the house
cleaned the bathrooms and
I still don't know how
to reverse the denial
that was scratched off my eyes
to get my OCD stimulated again

I'm stuck between knowing and action,
between too afraid to do anything and
too afraid to do nothing,
between the last time
I said I would and
the next phone call

I don't want to change
that bad
I can't go on living
this way

Is it a choice to get free
if it is the only other option
than sulking in the suffocating
of living in this body?

GRAMMAR CHECK

Now that Google has grammar check
in addition to spell check
I feel like a complete
failure of a writer

Never great with words
and the squiggly red and blue lines
patriotically remind me of it

One more instance
of society correcting me
One more validation of a story
I'm not smart enough
or worthy enough
to write well

One more suggestion
for a better way to say this
One more failing grade
One more try harder this time
so Mother will see you
so Grandma will see you
so Bubba can see you
so you can make it
in this pristine white world
One more pay attention
One more hurry up and listen
One more fall in line
One more dosage of normalcy

Grammar check,
no poetry
Spell check,

no magic
Behavior check,
no fun

Capital check
Whiteness check
Straightness check
Thinness check
Body check
Hair check
Ability check
IQ check
Girl check
Boy check
Health check
Perfection check

Grammar check
no poetry
Spell check,
no magic

Fail.

REPERCUSSIONS OF MANIA

The sound of my knee crunching
when I extend it,
lifting a box of rotten food
in my arms,
is the sound of my guilt
about a time long ago
that still exists
in my knees

Guilty for feeling guilty
Some things change
Repercussions of mania, linger

Like the extra weight I carry
from 20 years
of stories I added
to make sense of a world
that doesn't make sense,
that I tried to shed off
by running away

Wafting over,
like the smell
of this compost
These chores are a window
into a psychotic break I had 10 years ago

The mundane is never mundane
when we are
catching up to ourselves
from the past
when we were always running

SMOKING

I long for the inhale,
the sucking down,
the slow smokey release into the cold night
under stars and snowy trees,
the cloud of smoke that grabs onto
my hot breath
and I am dragon again

I miss not giving fucks
Being the bad one,
the one who talks of botchery
while they flick one more piece
of flakey mischief from their fingertips,
the one who cares more of satisfaction than death
the philosopher
the poet
the intellectual
the teenager
the lost one running, not trying to be found
except for in fleeting thoughts of a mother
the one who wants to be held by a mother
and knows it will never come

One more puff
in the name of defeat
in the name of life,
a dying thing

I miss the pain
of Saturday morning
after a night chain-smoking with my friends
talking on the porch
of all the dreams

falling from our pockets
with coins and the little piece of plastic
pulled off a new pack

I follow other people who
still have lips that can bear
the soft touch of the cotton,
who still have fingers
that can slide the paper
between them like that motion
they learned at 12, was yesterday
and I take a deep breath
to bring in the smoke
that was just in their lungs,
into mine,
trapped one more time
before it's finally free

I follow them with envy,
wondering if the voice of addiction
hasn't caught up and
gotten loud enough yet,
or that the voice of craving
still cranks out pushups
and gleams of power
I follow them like they
hold the secret answer to my anxiety,
knowing no secret still remains
on nicotine addiction

Most people know nicotine addiction
or are married to it
or are kin to it

I follow them because maybe
I could then convince myself of only one cigarette
at night, and on occasion

But I know I am addict
and what my existence entails
and most days I'm still searching
to breathe

IF MY HANDS WERE LESS DIRTY

If my hands were less dirty
I would hold you,
wrap you up like the last
piece of safety
you need before
you can fall apart

I would bundle you
in soft cheek kisses
and a mother's love
The last piece I saved,
to hold on to her
twenty years after
she left

If I wasn't so afraid
of how calloused my hands have become,
I would walk
hand in hand with you
right out of your home
into the front yard
surrounded
by elm
and cedar
and dogwood
and oak
and hemlock
and beech
and chestnut
and we would hide again

We would wander to the creek and catch
tiny fish in our hands,

only to let them go again
Stare at the tadpoles of the gopher frog,
swim until leeches
chase us out
and spend the next half hour
plucking them
from each other's
thin skin

I would carry you when you tire
I would walk with you when you want
power in your legs
I would tell you everything
I think you want to hear
because I know you won't ask for it,
because I know you barely speak
and I don't need
you to speak

We would wander past
the goats and chickens,
won't get chased out this time

On up the hill past
the red mailbox for your home
where we stored the car
on nights before a heavy snow

Left, down the long dirt road
past the house where
you only got apples on Halloween

Up the hill
where you fell
and skinned both your knees
while the horses stood watching

Past the church
where you ride
on your motorcycle-bike
in circles for hours
and hours
in escape

Beyond the patch
filled with four-leaf clovers
because you won't need
luck anymore

We run away instead

We will go back again,
when resourced enough
to fend for ourselves
When our armor
screams back,
It's not our fault

When our shields
hide the addiction
and only let the light come in
When we call magic beings
to enter
to protect
to erase
the time and start over again

We will return,
and you will have
your mother again

THEY

I love my pronouns so damn much
I forget they are not tattooed on my forehead,
that most people interpret my body as woman,
that they've been doing that to me since before I was born
I forget that my pronouns and my name
are the most sacred things
I've ever gifted myself
I forget how much work it took
allowing myself
that freedom,
how much work
it takes to maintain

I cannot believe that I lived long enough to meet the day
that I learned what a pronoun was,
what it means to have a language
to create a new world for my body,
what it means
to not be alone with that

Call me they
or sweetie
or darling
or them
or Hayden
or Hank
or honey
or their
Call me they over and over and over

MY FUTURE SELF

I cannot stop fantasizing about
my next T-shot
    the day that I'm man enough
    to grow my hair long
    and wear crop tops and sparkles
    The next T-shot won't get me there
    or the next one
    or the next one
    or the next one
    or the next one
    or the next one
    or the next one
    or the next one
    or the next one
    or the next one

    or the next one.

    I wake up obsessing about the girl
    I once was in the bathroom
    afraid of watching myself bleed
    as a sign of growing older

    Watching myself dying
    night after night
    from the poison
    too afraid to become
who I was before I bled

    I wake up obsessing about the needle
    Filling
    Too full
    Filling
    Air bubble
    Filling
    Ready
    Obsessing about the stabbing

Where I will stab next
How much it will hurt
Why it always has to hurt to become
How badly I want to breathe

I'm starved for my future self
I crave becoming
like how I used to crave escape

The whole point of the drugging
was to escape
The whole point of this needle
is to stay

I crave my future self
I crave my body
I crave to stay
I'm falling for my future self
I'm loving for today

III.

TONY

Despair took my tongue,
placed it neatly in a box
padded with gift wrap
sprinkled with candy,
taped it up and shipped it
to Tallahassee, FL
to Tony McDade's place
with a small note:

Please sir
use this as you must
Tell them who you were
Tell them the story
of how you were beaten
for living as yourself
Your trans body was your punishment
Your black body was your death sentence
Your heart was yours
not theirs to steal
Please sir
use this as you must

I slowly pull this needle out
Let its thin tip slide into the vile
Syringe squeezing freedom
Needle in thigh
His life helped me get here
My skin let me breathe
His life helped me arrive
Trancestor now

My ancestors were not migratory
they were fleeing persecution,

taught me what silence sounds like
The silence necessary to make the trauma disappear
Turned white in a lifetime,
finished it off with a good job
and a happy raging family
Gave me a world
where my early death could be my choice

White ancestors who watched lynchings
Must have had a million walls between their eyes and their guts
If you aren't crying today,
what of their walls do you still carry?

Take my tongue, say your name
Take my tongue, say your pronouns
Take my tongue, ship it back
when you're ready for me
to scream your name
for you too

There could be a world
where more Black trans leaders
are leading
Everyone else will be taken care of

It may not come soon
I will cry these walls away until it does

Tony
Tony
Tony
I'll scream until it does

THE SIZE OF MY GRIEF

I.

The way I carry myself has convinced them that I'm tall,
with the stretch of my neck,
pull of my shoulder,
I throw my hands up reaching
for a bar I set too high for myself
I could show you that I can grow to the size of my perfection so
you won't see
I actually grew to the size of my grief

I tried it on for size
even though not many things fit me,
even though these clothes weren't made for me,
even when my own skin doesn't fit me

A whomping five feet of body,
but I grew an extra inch of clever,
an extra inch of wit,
an extra inch of desperation,
an extra inch of survival

An extra inch for the times that the boys said
that if I wanted to play
I'd have to keep up,
didn't say that to the boys who couldn't keep up

An extra inch of bronze muscle
to prove to my mother I could be someone else,
pray to her god,
for him to just make me tall enough
so I could outgrow the part where I bleed like other girls do

These days I'd rather risk bleeding like other queers do
With every clip of my binder,
shoulders rolled back,
every gasp of my breath,
suffocating the girl out,
will drown my mother's voice out too,
and I want that most days
until it actually fades away
like her body,
like her ghost,
like my mind

When I grew that extra inch,
that time I sat stretched out
in the back seat of the cop car
Pulled between my father's grasp in the middle seat,
my forehead longing to be pressed against the glass

His weeping hug –
the kind of hug that wasn't for me,
the kind that kept my body still,
while his god pulled out a pocket lighter,
burned holes in my safety net

It's that kind of stillness,
where body stood paralyzed
while my drunk mother,
bloodshot eyes,
screamed final breaths over the body of her dead son

It was that extra inch
I grew in the dark parking lot that night
waiting outside of the hospital
when her hands were ripped from my hands
Stretched between her drunken gaze and my numb,
pulled between her desperation,

and someone else's will for me to survive that night
It was in that rapid growth
that night
that I convinced myself
to play small inside

II.

I watch myself outgrow this part:
the box that I made for myself
lined with barbed wire,
no trespassing signs,
guard dogs
and a secret entrance
The one that no longer fits,
nobody can tell me why

The one I know as a place already outgrown
so I can find the places
that I deserve to inhabit,
like a summer night under blankets of stars,
or a moving sidewalk under dancing feet,
or the space under a moon that won't stop watching
Like my softening gut
Like my own bones
filling with a mother's soft voice
reading me to sleep

My grief is not a fairy tale
It's a singing place
calling me to come home

If I were to actually grow to the size of my grief
I would grow to the size of
the search for my truth,
like a map to freedom in my skin,

or one step closer to letting my bones off the hook
or something that sounds dreamy
but certainly doesn't feel that way all the time

I would grow to the size of that itching thing
that I've felt for a while
but never had the courage to scratch;
never had the strength to reach hand to body
with every ounce of patriarchy's grip pulling it away

I would grow to the size of the one step forward I take
even with my mother's grief tied to my ankles
like that ball and chain I was gifted
as a forgotten child longing for freedom

I would grow to the size of what it would be like to breathe again
To let these binder straps wrap me
so tightly that the fabric begins to break,
and we unravel together in the softness of time

I would grow to the size of a utopia
that isn't a place but a process itself;
the very act of engaging in the tension of resistance

I'd grow to the size of the sweetness
in knowing, if even for a moment,
that there could be a day
where I feel understood,
or there could be a day where I don't have to

Even in the opacity of this world
there is love, and
maybe I don't have to be understood
to be loved, and
maybe I don't have to keep
adding inches of grief

because numbers become irrelevant when
time slips away and
the clock breaks,
and the ocean fade,
and I can breathe again
and I can grieve again

I won't grow to the size of my grief
I would just grow to the size of me,
this whomping five feet of body,
that has grown so strong
that finally
even my own broken heart
can't break it

FUNERAL

At my funeral
there will be
only cut lilies
as decoration
so that everyone
will spend their time wondering
almost entirely
about the cut lilies

How something so beautiful
could smell so bad;
how something
still living, can be dying,
or how something already dead
can still be living

How long the space in between
lasts for them as humans
How long it must feel for a lilly;
and if their perspective of
time even matters if
the process of death
is eternal
for every living one

If we are all just living things dying
or dying things still living
sped up by life
sped up by work
sped up by stress
sped up by fear
and fear
and fear

and fear

Their hands will touch
my face and they will
swallow the idea of me
Soak in the void
between the present
and anything in their mind
that could have happened
between us
Caught in the space
between reality
and dreams

And they will wonder
if it matters
or if it's all about their perspective,
if it's all about what they desire
And they will wonder
why they ever fed
anything but desire
and pleasure
and love
and hope
Why they did anything
but move towards justice,
demand another world,
smell flowers
uncut,
and pray

Kiss my forehead
and leave again
and begin again

FEBRUARY TENTH

If she were still alive
today she would
be turning 68
her hair would be
completely grey
Made it through
the greying stage, into
an old woman
with a crooked smile and
wrinkles down her arms
so large they could hide
every secret she ever
longed to keep,
every lie she ever
had on the backburner to
keep us in line

She would rant and rage
at the technology
these days;
the information left
at our fingertips, as if
Wikipedia exists
to disprove her clever stories
we couldn't seem to disprove
in the 90s

Now we know
we won't get worms from eating raw cookie dough,
or go blind if we fall asleep with our socks on,
or get our heads chopped off if we stick them out the car window,
or spell better with our fingers pointed straight up in the air,
but she would come up

with more ways to keep us
on our toes

She would take a deep sigh,
removing her glasses that have
thickened over time,
realizing that her
eyeliner is now on
her hands
because with exhaustion
came her tears
and wipes
and a simple
absent breath
over and over
throughout the day

She would look
back at the time
that she almost
didn't make it through,
as if it were not her life --
a fading memory from
when she wanted
to die
trapped in her cells
where addictions still
fail to remove themselves

She would wonder
how the miracle happened
What made her stay?
How god could possibly have
that much power
to make her not
turn the wheel

And she would fall
to her knees
on the evening
of her 68th birthday,
thank anything
that's listening
that she is okay

She would call me
her youngest child
just to apologize as if
it were yesterday,
and ask me
to come visit soon
regardless of the name change,
different pronouns
and new body --
to put it all aside and
come have tea for a while
to remind her why
she gave me life

She would softly swallow
her pride, a soft gulp
hidden under phone rattles,
a deep breath before
she finally
quietly
reminds me
how proud
she is
of all I am
becoming,
today

THE SKY'S NIGHT

It is my morning but
it is the sky's night
It is my obsession but
it is her life
and she is the one who lost it
She is the one
who wanders lost
in the liminal space left
I guess I am my mother's child

The only thing left
to separate us
is my flesh
and closed eyes
and stubborn mind
and calloused hands
and fragile bones
The only thing left
to tear me apart is myself

A broken heart
is only dangerous
to those who get close enough
to feel its sharp edges
as they reach for more
I never wanted
to inherit her burden
but I carry it
like her most loyal and only girl

I'm sorry some days
that my flesh carried
on for so long

without her
waiting for
anything more solid
than life

It's my morning but
it is the sky's night
It's my life
and I'm the one who lost it

TEMPORARY TATTOO

I ask you
if I look like
I'm healing,
as I stand
in front of you with
the remnants of
a temporary tattoo of
a shark eating
an ice cream cone,
clinging to my neck

Something designed
to be temporary,
and I'm still wondering
why I couldn't save it
Living in the regret of
why I didn't
design it to be
an ice cream cone
eating a shark

and why I always
ask you what
I already know

DYSPHORIA

I know you cannot see them
but I see them
and it's my body
and it's bad

I know you don't know
I almost drowned
in the bath
because I didn't run it hot enough to
keep my head up
My life is an accident
of a broken faucet

My hips stare me down
in the mirror again
I know my mother said one day this would happen
She said one day
I'd be trapped in a bathroom
wondering longingly at my hands,
how did it get this way?

I know I'm the gatekeeper to my essence
I know I'm the thought to my pain
I know that when I'm out of my mind
the magic comes in;
that the insane gets close enough
to smell it

I saw it in the back of a jar
that holds a candle
that lights a room

only enough to remind me
I'm alive
but not enough to show me my hips

NARCOTICS

The just in case drugs
The easily justifiable
cabinet fillers
The post-expiration
emergency-only bottle
Top-shelf
Label backwards
Not to be touched
Little safety vests
Tiny soft pillows
for my crooked neck and stained smile
For the extra dazed sleep
if the pain ever gets too bad

Sober for enough years
that they are about
to slip from my fingers
crouched on the bathroom floor
and I still hold them
like a last chance
at getting off the hook early
An easy out
A fallen star
A proved-you-wrong
I'm-not-so-good-after-all moment
A hopeless child
A fuck you for putting faith in me
An apology
A fantasy

A fantasy for the days
I just don't want to stay

even though
I stayed every day
for 30 years

A joke
that's not funny
now
that I've reached
the other side of numb

Now
that I've seen enough
felt enough
cared enough
Now that you care
Now that I matter

Now
that I could write
an entire book
of minor miracles
and call it serenity

Now
that life
is not a thing
to exchange
like the drugs were

a gamble for a high
a risk for an escape

Now
that the world goes on
whether I'm in it
or not

Now that you matter
Now that I care

Bottle down
Once

upon a time
I changed

IV.

YOUR OTHER PALM EXTENDED

I've been walking through this jungle thicket
I've got vines wrapped
around my arms
my knees are deep in mud
I'm trudging my way back through
the stories I've created to survive
wondering how things ended up this way –
nothing has always been this way

You're standing here before me,
machete reached out in one hand for me to take it,
your other palm extended
to my empty one
I close my eyes in disbelief
I open them
You're still there
I stand here paralyzed

I know every breath has become
one more step,
every pause a space for
me to wonder
If only you knew
the way my bones boil,
if you knew these caves and these cliffs,
how we navigate the dark patches,
how my blood reeks with inauthenticity,
my throat closes
around the truth hidden
in the depths of my mind
drowned by the sound
of whiskey cannons,
if only you knew

But you know
so there's nothing left to do but let go,
breaking empty bottles and
empty modes of operation
Because I keep heading
back to the bar that
I've set so high for myself,
buying drinks for my own loneliness to
drown the sound of
"everything will always be this way,"
Nothing has always been this way

So I wait with
clenched fists wrapped
around a wrinkled up
piece of paper with "Wild Geese" scratched on to it
reminding me I don't have to
walk on my knees repenting

As vacant thoughts fly
out the back door
I lay trapped in two worlds navigating
the space between
what's real and what could be
I take the machete laid before me

It's time to strike down the sound
of broken stories
telling me, "everything will always be this way"
Nothing has always been this way

So I pray because
acceptance doesn't come so easily
but she is hiding behind me whispering
in my ear, "just let go," she says,

"just let go"

Surrender doesn't come so easily,
I close my eyes in disbelief
I open them
You're still there

ON NIGHTS AS FOGGY AS THIS

I.

On nights as foggy as this I can't tell
where the fog ends and
my ghosts begin but
I can feel them breathing
I can hear their whispers softly singing
I can smell the remanence of
broken hearts and
regrets gone stale

I know they are there because I remember
when they left for a while
I remember
when my panic
needed rest
and I lost them
in the breeze they stopped
haunting me,
until I went searching and
begged them to keep me
up at night

Now on nights as foggy as this we play
melodies on repeat,
dance in fields where
nobody can see
We play games of make-believe
pretend
I am a child
They are alive

I am a child again

I have bones of solid iron
so strong the words won't break me
so strong the bottle won't break me
so strong the fists won't break me
I become invisible
I hide the coke and the gun in the back of the closet where
I know they won't go because
the monsters won't let them in
and they are angry,
but I can hide
I am a child
They are alive

On nights as foggy as this we build fires
They creep through old hallways
I write half poems that
I wish told me
the answers to my grief
Instead they tell me
it's not a question
I burn them

I pray that the next poem that comes out whole
has the answers to my grief
Instead, it tells me that
my grief
is not a question
I burn it

Because some days god
is just the blackness of the night
and writing is just the answer
and seeking is just the end
and hauntings will be
and I won't remember where
their bones lay but

I know they will guide me to
their grave one day

II.

On nights as foggy as this we get lost
in the smell of old books and mother's clothes
We tell stories of what
we imagined life to be,
we take turns dreaming

On nights as foggy as this I realize
that I'm crying
when the tears roll down my wrist
my head held up by other bones,
and they will weep for having no bones
and we will take turns dreaming
and I will ask them to hold me
and they will weep for having no bones

On nights as foggy as this
I touch tongues with my grief,
hide the shackles I used to chain it down
I hold hands with my ghosts
as we caress the insurmountable inside
that claims this is
just what it is to be human
while it stands in the doorway of the entrance
to god

I desperately search for the secret password
the hidden weapons
the golden key
until she whispers at me, "quiet child, we must go now"
They slip away into the clouds
The moon comes out

Yet I am a child
They are alive

WILL YOU SEE ME?

Mother,

If you could see me today would you see me?
Would you let me be me?
Would you say you've always known or
be shocked with disappointment?
Would you hold me?
Would you love me?
Would you grieve the idea of me
before giving me
your grief?
Would you walk through the opacity
that exists between us?

Hands out
Move slow

Would you find me?

My genderless body?
Would you pull it closer to you despite
the heat that rises from the fire inside?
Would you use it to stay warm instead of hide?
Do you remember how my fire burned?
How it grew
from ashes to flame,
and how the uncontrollable rage left us
both burnt out?
And when you picked up that liquor bottle,
how the house went up in flames?
Would you let me burn today?

My body was not born
a political statement,
it was born into a world that made it one
You prayed, "not a son"
Your dying tradition,
your rising addiction
would be covered if
I could just be
perfect this time

Your perfect girl
who sings melodies so sweet
even the birds fall in love

When you gave me my gender
before giving me my name,
did you know we would go up in flames?

Tied to your genes
were your visions
you passed on to me
Did you know
my truth could be
different than yours?
Or did you just have no other tongue?

Without language we have no choice
Only assimilation or a barbed wire paddle
A flower dress or an eternity in hell
A boyfriend or a beatdown
A value system or another mother walking out the door

Are you a boy or a girl? Are you a boy or a girl? Are you a boy or
a girl? Are you a boy or a girl? Are you a boy or a girl? Are you a
boy or a girl? Are you a boy or a girl? Are you a boy or a girl?

Which side are you on?
Why do you hide behind lockers?
Why don't you come swim with us?
Are you a boy or a girl? Are you a boy or a girl? Are you a boy or
a girl? Are you a boy or a girl?
they would say

I was lost in my mind
for more days than I was there
I tried to answer
I stared at my body
I was gone again

You were gone again
You went to rehab again,
to the hospital again,
to your abuser again,
back to rehab again,
to the hospital again,
back to rehab again

Mother,
I'll wear the dress
just don't leave again

Mother,
I tried to be perfect
so you would return home
from your death,
tell me
it wasn't actually real

I stored all of these
hauntings inside of me
I just can't be your perfect body
because I swept

so many skeletons under the rug
that my queerness came
out the other side and
it's hard not to notice
an open wound on this body that has
no answers, only truth

This body once flames,
once yours,
once inside of you

If I gave you a language would you
let it melt on your tongue?
If I gave you a choice would you
hold it close to your heart like
you once held my name?
Would you dance not knowing
who would dance with you?
Would you dance with me to?
Would you wish upon stars you know don't exist anymore
simply because you think their answers do?
Would you pray for me or with me?
Would you lay awake on sleepless nights
because of me, or beside of me?
Would you throw your body at me, or in front of me?
Would you smother me,
or let me burn today?

Would you hold me?

Mother?

COYOTE

I've been watching you
coyote, move
through these hills,
breaking open the veil that
binds our silence,
tearing through normalcy like
enough flesh for one more day
I've been watching you
trickster, running away
mischievous smile on your face

I hope to become you one day
to fully embody the grey space
in between worlds
in both desire and in fear

We can never fully abandon the past
Untangling from the trauma
that glued my lips together
takes more than a good pry
Untangling from supremacy
that puffed up my chest
takes more than a heavy sigh

But I'll surrender in the name of justice
I'll pause in the name of urgency
I'll fail in the name of last chances
I'll grieve in the name of crisis
I'll grieve over and over again
until I have nerves for skin
Come closer and hold my hand
until the collapse arrives

It all began with tragedy
so it can only end with hope
and bloom again
from the ashes of our bones
A sweet mystery to come
May my body be grounds for you
coyote, to dance upon

SHRINE

On the days that I'm thinking
"holy hell is it actually possible to get through anything together?"
I remember how far we have come,
how much we have grown,
how we longed for connection
but had to remember that the path
towards it is through
breaking every bone of resistance
we built up to save our faces
a long time ago

I hope my ego crumbles at the sight of you
every day of our lives
until we are old
and have no fight in us left
except the one for love and justice

I remember how much we dream
of safety and security and love
of dance parties and performance art
of playing Celion Dion's "My Heart Will Go On" on repeat at
our wedding
Can't stop laughing
and it's easy again
to know anything is possible,
to know healing only happens in connection,
to know we are not only getting through,
but hitching rides on one another's backs
as fast as we can
when we need to
and holding hands
through the slow and painful parts

One day at a time
flies by sometimes
I hope I savor every breath
in the shrine of our love
we call our home

QUEERING LOVE

I once saw a hand-painted sign
in a gazebo that said,
Fill yourself with love so doubt cannot get in

I don't want to be filled with love
so that doubt cannot get in
I want to be filled with love
so that I can feel
everything again

Love is not the absence of doubt,
love is its mother
I want my love to
nourish doubt
befriend doubt
sing doubt
a soft melody
to fall
asleep at night

I hear time and time again that
one person completes the other
but what if we are all actually already complete?
What if what we really meant was that
one person provides space
for the other
to fully and safely express themself?
And in that action
we move
towards ourselves
and one another

And we embrace ourselves
in a world that taught us
to drown before trying
And so with self-love we can breathe again,
with the exhale we can give more back
Maybe that
is what it means
to be complete

I once heard in a song
"I can be your hero, baby"
And I hear in so many songs that
love is just about finding a savior
but what if we didn't need to be saved?
What if we had every answer
to every question
and love just taught us
to keep asking more?

What if we weren't born
to be with someone
but were born
to love ourselves
amongst everyone?

What if it's just the thing that
helps us stay
in the liminal space?
One solid foot in this world
and one on the other side,
the clasp of our hands
squeezing so tight
for the days that we are smothered
by capitalism,
we can at least feel
that we are also smothered by love

and wait for the panic
to slip from our fingers
when we finally let go

Maybe it's knowing that all truth is change
Maybe it's accepting that all change is in motion
It's feeling everything
All of this world's pain
All of this bleeding heart
All of this joy
All of this laughter
so intense that your cheeks are sore
It's lovers,
and friends,
and family
It's blood by choice
It's always having a choice
It's choosing another life again today

It's falling in love
with the dangling moss
on the lodgepole pine,
the quiet weight of the forest,
the raging South St. Vrain in early summer,
the crackling of the leaves dying in the fall,
the moments of being
completely alone
and knowing you're still held, never alone
It's loving being completely alone

It's being more
alive every day
we step closer
to death
together
It's walking around fields to pick bouquets

of dead things
because the already dead
lasts longer than
the soon to die

It's deciding to not just let ourselves die
because we matter,
because we are cared for and
can see it every day
now in the eyes
of people who reflect
this deepest feeling back
It's realizing that our deepest feelings are shared,
are human

It's fucking up,
over and over
and over again
and having someone to tell us
we are worth the battle of healing
That healing happens
in connection
and that we are okay
It's realizing that apart we are okay
and together we are okay & okay

I've heard people say you are supposed to love one gender
I've heard people say you can love whoever you want
It's all as if loving were a choice,
as if queerness were a choice,
as if this body could breathe
without love,
without expression,
as if brains could ponder
anything but magic
as if love were not magic

I don't want love
to block anything out
so long as the
magic can still get in
and do what it will
with the rest

ANCESTOR TO BE

I.

You couldn't be there in life,
so find me in death
Love, not as noun
but as verb
Love, not as feeling
but the act of extension,
the pursuit of self-reflection,
the genius of unlearning
Love me as I needed to be loved
now that your skin can't box you in

Your fire was fierce
I know because I carry it with mine
Falling into flames,
rage seeping from my pores,
love pounding from my heart,
fear oozing from the scars I left
behind punched walls and quick regrets
A cheap merlot and a pack of cigarettes would have taken the
edge off too
but I gave them up
to not become a young corpse like you
burnt out too soon

I see now how you were always running
I would have traded anything
to keep you in flesh
I see now I cannot sacrifice myself
to keep those in flesh
who cannot hold all of me
but I am afraid of that truth --

Help me hold all of it

Love me in your freedom
from your limiting breath
Love me in your expansion
The love you still carry

II.

Death makes life
makes death makes
life makes death
makes life makes
death

To know is not the same as acceptance
To understand is not the same as feeling
Year after year I watched the leaves change on the trees
hovering over their graves
praying fall would never come again

It's not her secrets I remember, but the confusion
It's not her words I know, but the language of my gut
How I betrayed myself to survive
my whole life
blinded by gaslights
passed through generations
still treading through this murky life

The secrets are hers but they live in my body
stored with memories and trauma
in a small box
locked away with a key
held by no one

No power to access them
Power only to change my story over time
knowing what I know comes from my body
not my mind

The truth is not a weapon, but I can use it as one
The truth is not gold, but I'll devote my nights
searching for my own
My life's work is
slowly untangling from my formative years
spent in the cobweb of her lies
I've bound myself with
so my body,
ancestor to be,
brings peace

Not adding more of my own lies
will have to be work
for the afterlife

I hope my ghost carries clarity
to the future generations
learning to unlearn
resisting to live
fighting to survive
for our collective liberation --
theirs and mine
so we can all taste freedom
in death and life

I hope my ghost caries all the love
like she does now
to bring hope
to the moments between grief
so all can touch harmony,
wrap ourselves in belonging

ACKNOWLEDGMENTS

These poems were written on unceded territory of Hinóno'éí (Arapaho), Nuutsiu (Ute) and Tsitsistas (Cheyenne) Nations and home to many Native Peoples today. The experiences of these poems took place on colonized Aniyvwiya?i (Cherokee) land, in a place built with stolen lives, labor and love of black people. May reparations come soon. May the healing of repair be a blessing to all.

Thank you to:

Al and Ruckus, my family, loves, best friends, and favorite pillows

Caleb and Pops, for getting us through

The ghosts who love me in this flesh

The ones in flesh who love me before I become ghost

The ones who offered new stories

Blake, for editing and for teaching me line breaks and other ways
of smearing words around on a page to make them look
pretty

Karolina, for being my number one fan and coming to all of my
shows

Staff at Atmosphere Press, for all of the work of making these
words become physical

The ones who read the words

The ones who breathe the words

ABOUT ATMOSPHERE PRESS

Atmosphere Press is an independent, full-service publisher for excellent books in all genres and for all audiences. Learn more about what we do at atmospherepress.com.

We encourage you to check out some of Atmosphere's latest releases, which are available at Amazon.com and via order from your local bookstore:

River, Run!, poetry by Caitlin Jackson
Canine in the Promised Land, poetry by Philip J. Kowalski
The Heroin Addict's Mother, a memoir in poetry by Miriam Greenspan
Golden Threads, poetry by Uranbileg Batjargal
Poems for the Asylum, poetry by Daniel J. Lutz
This Woman is Haunted, poetry by Betsy Littrell
Quitting Time, poetry by Patrick Cabello Hansel
all the things my mother never told me, poetry by Daniella Deutsch
The Distance from Odessa, poetry by Carol Seitchik
How It Shone, poetry by Katherine Barham
Wind Bells, poetry in English and Tagalog by Jessica Perez Dimalibot
Meraki, poetry by Tobi-Hope Jieun Park
Impression, poetry by Charnjit Gill
Aching to be Human, poetry by Stormy Abel
Love is Blood, Love is Fabric, poetry by Mary De La Fuente
How to Hypnotize a Lobster, poetry by Kristin Rose Jutras
The Mercer Stands Burning, night poems by John Pietaro
Calls for Help, poetry by Greg T. Miraglia
Lost in the Greenwood, poetry by Ellen Roberts Young
Lovely Dregs, poetry by Richard Sipe
Shadow Truths, poetry by V. Rendina
Big Man Small Europe, poetry by Tristan Niskanen
Lucid_Malware.zip, poetry by Dylan Sonderman
The Unordering of Days, poetry by Jessica Palmer
Radical Dances of the Ferocious Kind, poetry by Tina Tru

Hayden Dansky is a transgender nonbinary rural Jewish queer kid trying their best to not to be smothered by capitalism. They have been writing and performing poetry for several years, and are currently collaborating with local experimental musicians and dancers to create performances that encompass multiple disciplines. Their most recent written work can be found in *Bible Belt Queers, Thought for Food, South Broadway Ghost Society Online Journal,* and *Spit Poet Volume 8.* They are also the Executive Director of Boulder Food Rescue, a nonprofit working to create a more just and less wasteful food system, through the sustainable redistribution of healthy food and participatory and community-led food access systems.

CPSIA information can be obtained
at www.ICGtesting.com
Printed in the USA
FSHW012326040621
81984FS